**Now You Know Science**

# Bright Light

## Terry Jennings

FRANKLIN WATTS
LONDON • SYDNEY

This edition 2013

First published in 2009 by Franklin Watts

Franklin Watts
338 Euston Road, London NW1 3BH

Franklin Watts Australia
Level 17/207 Kent St, Sydney, NSW 2000

Copyright © Franklin Watts 2009

Created by Taglines Creative Ltd: Jean Coppendale and Honor Head
Written by: Terry Jennings
Design: Paul Manning

ISBN: 978 1 4451 2321 9

Dewey classification: 535

A CIP catalogue for this book is available from the British Library.

Picture credits
t=top  b=bottom  l=left  r=right

3, 8, Karen Struther, Shutterstock; 5, 20, 29tr, Felix Casio; 6, Holger Mette, Shutterstock;
7, Thomas Sztanek, Shutterstock; 9, Jorge Salcedo, Shutterstock; 10, 28b, Igor Marx, Shutterstock;
11, Rajesh Pattabiraman, Shutterstock; 12, 28tr, Yan Zenkis, Shutterstock; 13, Mike Flippo,
Shutterstock; 14, Agafon, Shutterstock; 15, Anna Dzondzua, Shutterstock; 16, Kamyshko,
Shutterstock; 17, 28tl, Donald Joski, Shutterstock; 18, Coko, Shutterstock; 19, Sascha Burkard,
Shutterstock; 21, Anyka, Shutterstock; 22, 29tl, Tadija, Shutterstock; 23, 29bl, Stuart Monk,
Shutterstock; 24, Carsten Reisinger, Shutterstock; 25, Blazej Maksym, Shutterstock;
26, Wael Hamdan, Shutterstock; 27, Evan66, Shutterstock.

Printed in China

Franklin Watts is a division of Hachette Children's Books, an Hachette UK company.
www.hachette.co.uk

# Contents

# Light and dark

The sun gives us lots of bright light in the daytime.

▼ **During the day we get light from the sun.**

At night, when the sun is not shining, it is dark.

▲ **When there is no sun we need other sorts of light to help us see.**

# The sun

On a clear summer's day, the sun can be very bright and hot.

**STOP!**
**Never look at the sun. It is so bright it will hurt your eyes.**

▲ **When the sun is very bright, you should wear sunglasses.**

On days when it is wet and cloudy, the sun is not very bright.

 **Even when we cannot see the sun, we still get some light from it.**

# Electric lights

When it is dark, we use electric lights on the streets and in our homes.

▲ **Electric lights are not as bright as the sun.**

At home, we use lots of different electric lights to help us see at night.

▲ **How many electric lights can you see in this picture?**

# Fire light

Fire is hot. A fire can also be used to give us light.

The bigger the fire, the brighter the light it will give out.

The small flames on candles do not give out much light.

▲ Candles look pretty, but we need a lot of candles to make a bright light.

# Seeing light

You see light with your eyes. Light goes into each eye through a small 'hole' called the pupil.

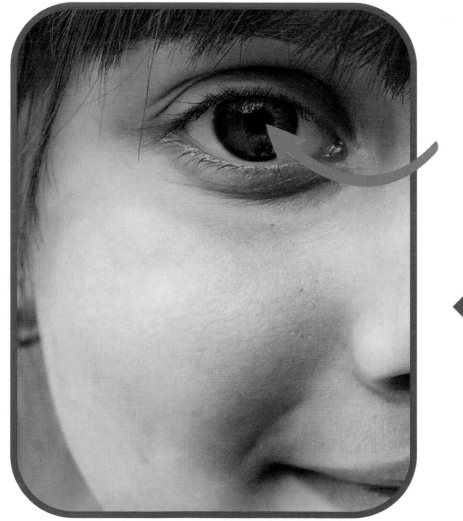

pupil

In dim light your pupils get bigger to let in more light.

When the light is very bright, you might need to shade your eyes to see.

 **In bright light your pupils get smaller, so less light goes into your eyes.**

# Shining through

Light shines through a window.
A window is made from glass.

▲ **Trains have lots of windows so you can see where you are going.**

Some materials let light through, but you cannot see through the material.

lampshade

▲ You can see the light from the light bulb but you cannot see the bulb through the lampshade.

# Blocking the light

Some materials do not let any light through.
Light cannot go through bricks or wood.
They block out the light.

glass

wall

▲ **You can see through the glass in the window but you cannot see through the wall.**

Materials you can see through are called transparent. Materials you cannot see through are called opaque.

▲ **What would this house be like inside if it did not have any windows, only bricks?**

# Shadows

Light travels in straight lines. It cannot bend around things. If something gets in the way of light, it makes a shadow.

shadow

shadow

▲ **When you are in the way of the sun's light, you make a shadow.**

You can make shadows indoors using
a torch or table lamp.

**shadow**

**light from a torch**

 **These shadows are made by shining a torch
on the paper figures.**

# Reflection

When light hits a smooth, shiny surface it bounces back. It makes a reflection.

▲ **A mirror is smooth and shiny. When you look in a mirror, you can see your reflection.**

When water is smooth and shiny, it can make reflections like a mirror.

▲ **This ladybird's reflection in the water is upside down. Why do you think the reflection is broken up?**

# Coloured lights

Light can be different colours. Traffic lights are three different colours.

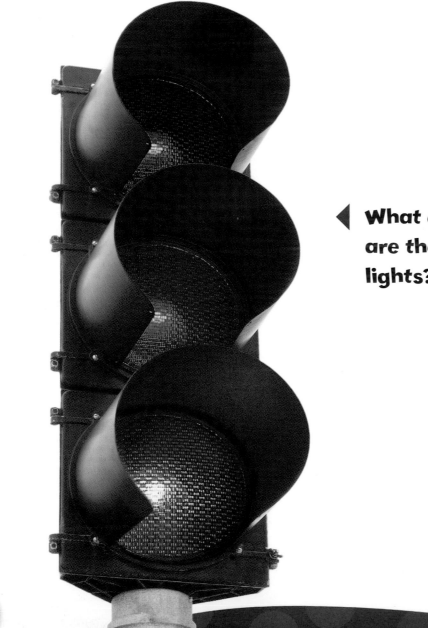

**What colours are these traffic lights?**

When it rains and the sun shines, we often see a rainbow.

▲ **Have you seen a rainbow like this? What colours can you see in this rainbow?**

# Plants need light

Plants need light and water to grow strong and healthy.

▲ **These plants have had lots of sun and rain.**

Without light, plants do not grow properly. They become weak and their leaves turn yellow and die.

▲ **This plant has not had much light or water.**

# Things to do

## Lots of light

What different types of light can you see here?

a

b

c

# Odd one out

Which pictures show a reflection?
What is making a shadow?

a

b

c

# Talk back

What is the weather like today?
Is it sunny and bright, or cloudy?
What electric lights can you see
near you now?

# Glossary

**electric light** A light that uses electricity. It has to be switched on and off.

**light bulb** A glass bulb that can be switched on to make light.

**opaque** When you cannot see through an object.

**shade** To cover something from bright light.

**transparent** When you can see through an object.

# Index